Whispers of Rest in the Storm

Matthea Browning Glass

Energion Publications
Gonzalez, FL
2019

Copyright © 2019, Matthea Browning Glass

All Scripture quotations, unless otherwise indicated, are taken from the Holy Bible, New International Version®, NIV®. Copyright ©1973, 1978, 1984, 2011 by Biblica, Inc.™ Used by permission of Zondervan. All rights reserved worldwide. www.zondervan.com The "NIV" and "New International Version" are trademarks registered in the United States Patent and Trademark Office by Biblica, Inc.™

The cover image is a painting by the author. All interior illustrations are from Pixabay.com.

ISBN10: 1-63199-687-8
ISBN13: 978-1-63199-687-0
Library of Congress Control Number: 2019940513

Energion Publications
P. O. Box 841
Gonzalez, FL 32560

energionpubs.com
pubs@energion.com
850-525-3916

Dedicated to my children

Katherine, Carter, Caleb, Christian, Kai, and Karis-Lynn

Through...

Through the storm,
A whisper.
Through the night,
A shaft of light.
Lingering there in the heavy air,
A promise.
This is not the end.
A beginning dancing,
Just out of sight.

Introduction

    This devotional is written for anyone who needs to learn to rest. Our nature protests rest, especially in times of upheaval. We must make a deliberate, conscience choice to walk in the Spirit by learning to rest in God. This is true for the business woman, the new mom, the woman recovering from abuse, and the addict.

    Ever since Eve took the forbidden fruit in hand, we have been working to make our lives better and avoid any kind of disturbance by taking the wide path of the generations that came before us. Like Eve, we staunchly resist God's way. Think how different the world would look if Eve had said, "No! Satan, the fruit does look good enough to eat. But … I'm going to rest in the truth that God is bigger than me, and He knows the reason that we shouldn't touch the fruit even if I don't."

    Come along and take a deep breath with me. Each day for the next month learn to rest in God's truth. As I walked through the valley of darkness after the death of my son, I found God's rest. He whispered truth to my soul in the storm of grief. Much of my sorrow in my storm flowed from unbelief or wrong beliefs. I found that God is more loving and compassionate than I can ever comprehend. Now, I am even more convinced that He wants to make Himself known to me and save me from all my troubles. I learned that I need to humble myself and say, "Lord, I don't know why, but I'm going to rest in the truth that You are bigger than me, and You know more than me. I can trust that You are good. You are Love, and I can trust in You, even in the messy middle."

The storm you face may be different but come along with me and learn that rest is more than inactivity or ceasing work or movement. During hardships we learn that rest is learning to refresh oneself in the truth of Scripture, rather than our feelings and recovering our strength in the Lord, when we are overwhelmed. My prayer is that throughout this time of rest for your soul, you will find refreshing truths, recover your strength in areas you are weak, and cease working to be good enough for Jesus, your family, and yourself. Learn to rest in God's rest.

In Christ,
Matthea Browning Glass

Day 1

Rest in a Prayer of Renewal

We are asking that you may be filled with the knowledge of His will in all wisdom and spiritual understanding so that you may walk worthy of the Lord, fully pleasing to Him, bearing fruit in every good work and growing in the knowledge of God. May you be strengthened with all power, according to His glorious might, for all endurance and patience with joy, giving thanks to the Father, who has enabled you to share in the saints' inheritance in the light. He has rescued us from the domain of darkness and transferred us into the kingdom of the Son He loves, in whom we have redemption, the forgiveness of sins. Colossians 1:9-14

Pray through these verses everyday this month. This prayer in Colossians teaches us to know or to be aware of these truths through demonstration, not by how we feel about what is written. One of the very reasons we need to learn to rest is *because of our feelings*. In the middle of a storm our feelings tell us what the storm is like not what we should do about it. God created feelings for a purpose. They help us interact with the world around us. They help us to love deeply. They alert us to danger. Feelings are a thermometer. They give us the temperature; that's it. How we feel about a situation does not give us a solution to the situation. Maybe our feelings are telling us that the situation has become unmanageable. The next step is to ask God for wisdom. We can feel very strongly and still be very wrong, but God's way is never wrong. We must ask Him to fill us with His wisdom. When we learn to rest in God, He clothes us with all wisdom and spiritual understanding so that we may walk worthy of the Lord. What our flesh (feelings) is unable to do, God does through His mercy and grace in Jesus.

Today, we may not feel strong. Learning to rest in this prayer of renewal, leads us to wait for the Lord to strengthen us with His power. Stop trying to accomplish anything through willpower. He will give us endurance and patience with joy, but we can only live one day at a time. If we carry yesterday's hurts and tomorrow's

worries, we will be exhausted. God gives us strength for one day at a time, sometimes moment by moment.

If we find that we are carrying yesterday's hurts, we need to expose them to the Light. Hurts do not heal with time. When we stuff hurts into the basement of our hearts that hurt becomes foundational to our identity. We subconsciously respond to the world around us out of that hurt. God's truth is that He has rescued us from the domain of darkness. We may not feel rescued from these hurts, but in Christ Jesus we are. Because of Jesus, we have been transferred to the Kingdom of the Son, who the Father loves! Though the storms of this life are blindingly dark, make a conscience choice to believe God will give all wisdom and spiritual knowledge for today.

What hurts do you need to bring to the Light today? What worries can you lay down? Remember this is a process of taking one step of faith at a time, and the Spirit takes every step with you.

Rest because you know that you have been transferred from darkness into the Kingdom of Light.

Day 2

Rest in the Crucifixion

For we know that our old self was crucified with Him in order that sin's dominion over the body may be abolished, so that we may no longer be enslaved to sin. Romans 6:6

We should share the Good News of the Gospel with ourselves daily. Every day brings its own evil that we must face. As I rest in the truth that I died with Jesus on the cross, I know that the power of sin has been broken. Please pause to ponder on how different the word "know" is from the word "feel." There are times I do not feel dead to sin, but I am!

Here's a little of what I say to myself.

Although, I fall short of God's glory all the time, I am justified freely by His grace through the redemption that came by Jesus Christ. It's not by works or achievement or who my parents are.

I am so thankful that I can be as patient with my healing and growth as Jesus is with His disciples. Even when I am cold and irritable with my family, I thank Jesus for being patient and tender. In Luke 22, just before the crucifixion, Jesus asks the disciples to pray while He went to pray. When He returned, they were asleep. Jesus was gentle, I can be that too.

The Power of sin is broken!

    If we acted out of a certain attitude or a behavioral pattern for most of our lives, deep change will take time. No one gets to skip this step. We humble ourselves and ask God's forgiveness for the sinful way we have lived. We do this with grace and mercy because we rest in the crucifixion! We are forgiven, not because we've learned to act right, but because of Jesus's perfect work on the cross.

Let the above truth sink in deep. The beauty of faith is that our faith doesn't break the power of sin. The completed work has already done so. We are simply raising our hand and telling God we want Him to apply it to us. As we walk in this truth our belief becomes action by living in freedom instead of under the compulsion to continue in old patterns of behavior that brought us pain. Spend some time thinking about one thought or behavioral pattern that is hurtful and apply the grace of Jesus to it. Write out a prayer incorporating the gospel. Start with, "I fall short of God's glory, but I am freely justified through Christ!"

> *Rest in the crucifixion today. Replace a sinful behavioral pattern with how Jesus demonstrated a new way to live. Remember that He paid the price, He covered that sin with His blood. Rest in your death on the cross with Jesus Christ!*

Day 3

Rest in Forgiveness

Therefore, I tell you, her many sins have been forgiven; that's why she loved much. But the one who is forgiven little, loves little. Luke 7:47

For most of us the idea that our many sins can be forgiven is incompatible with reason. I know what I have done. You know what you have done. We are more familiar with punishment and condemnation.

Many Christians continue to carry around feelings of shame and defeat from our sinful past. Sometimes in unbelief we continue to flog ourselves with this past to pay the debt we think we deserve. God is a just, a merciful, and a grace-filled Father. Justice is when God gives us what we deserve. In His mercy, He sent Jesus to take upon Himself the sins of the whole world, satisfying His wrath, *giving to Jesus what we deserved*. Grace is when God gives us what we don't deserve, forgiveness. God knew that we could never pay our debts, so He did it for us! Why do we now think that we can make ourselves right by beating ourselves up, by condemning ourselves in our thoughts, or by punishing ourselves by how we live?

The truth is that we don't deserve forgiveness. But, if someone wanted to give us a gift of a million dollars, would we refuse it? Would we keep carrying around our poverty with the gift of great wealth sitting there? Accepting Jesus as Lord and Savior is accepting His gift of forgiveness. Learning to rest in His forgiveness is allowing the old failures to be buried with Christ (Romans 6:4) and living in the reality that we are raised with Christ to live a new life (Romans 6:10).

Sometimes we continue to battle feelings of guilt and shame because we have not asked others for forgiveness and worked to make amends for the wrong we did. Proverbs 14:9 says, "Only fools mock at making amends, but good will is found among the upright." Making amends doesn't pay for our wrongs; they demonstrate our true repentance.

Sometimes we battle feelings of guilt and shame because we must expose old hurts to the Light. Some stories need to be shared in order to heal. Allowing the Light into our deepest hurts exposes them to the truth. We are not innately bad and deserve abuse.

Someone sinned against us. Let that person own her/his sin. We can stop carrying it, if we give it to Jesus. We have carried the secret for long enough. Telling Jesus is the first step to finding healing. He knows it. On the cross the weight of every sin was laid on Him. The weight of our secret was already laid on Him on the cross (Isaiah 53). He took it, and paid for it with His blood. Now it's up to us to put it down and let Him carry it.

Learning to rest in forgiveness will free us from the bondage of working for salvation. When we know we are forgiven, we can love much because we know that we are forgiven much. God's forgiveness is not reasonable to people who cannot pay for their sins, but Isaiah 53:10 says that it pleased the Lord to crush Jesus for our redemption.

Let's stop condemning ourselves for what God has forgiven, especially since that forgiveness spilt the blood of Christ Jesus. One definition of rest is to cease work or movement.

Learning to rest in forgiveness is allowing Jesus to carry the weight of sin. Let us cease trying to earn forgiveness and rest in the forgiveness given by living "In Christ."

Day 4

Rest in Reconciliation

> *Therefore if anyone is in Christ, there is a new creation; old things have passed away, and look, new things have come. Now everything is from God, who reconciled us to Himself through Christ and gave us the ministry of reconciliation.*
> 2 Corinthians 5:17-18

Oh! How beautiful is the work of Jesus Christ for us! Two things happen when we come to faith in Christ. Positional reconciliation and experiential reconciliation. "We who believe the gospel are now experiencing the beginning of salvation's benefits, but we will not know the full blessings until our resurrection" (*A Theology for the Church*, Danny Akin).

Positional reconciliation occurs at salvation and experiential reconciliation is a life-long process. Ephesians 1:3 assures us that our salvation is a finished reality, and Philippians 2:12-13 emphasizes the ongoing work of reconciliation.

The struggles we now have are with the patterns of behavior that we had prior to salvation. Slowly the Lord increases His spotlight of faith. He digs deeper and deeper into our hearts to root out indwelling sin, so that we can enjoy Him more and more. We grow to love Him more and more as we continue to lay aside our desires, pick up His will for our lives, and accomplish the good works that He set out for us to do (Ephesians 2:10)!

My husband uses the analogy of a wedding to explain positional and relational reconciliation. After the bride and groom say their vows, they are married, but they don't go home in different cars to different houses. They live together, growing more and more in love with one another as the years go by.

We should look at our salvation like a marriage. As we learn to trust, our faith will grow, and relationally, we grow closer to the Lord as we understand more about His nature, His character, and His acts. As we walk with God, "He transforms us into his image with ever-increasing glory, which comes from the Lord, who is the Spirit" (2 Corinthians 3:18). This transformation is the process of experiential reconciliation. The difficult truth to grapple with is that we must walk through many griefs, adversities, and troubles to experience the reality of God's reconciliation. Our faith in what we know to be true often grows through the storms we endure rather than times of comfort.

This was true for Job. Only after he experienced the death of his children, loss of his wealth, the persecution by his friends', and his many sicknesses did he proclaim, "My ears had heard of you, but now my eyes have seen you" (Job 42:5).

> *Even though we may be frustrated or impatient because we experience troubles, temptations, and failures. We know for sure that our sins are forgiven. We rest in the reconciliation brought by salvation, but we must still journey through this broken world as a witness, being careful not rebel against the way that God has chosen to display His mercy in us to those who are far away from Him.*

Day 5

Rest in your Adoption

Because you are his sons, God sent the Spirit of his Son into our hearts, the Spirit who calls out, "Abba, Father." Galatians 4:6

During times of distress, feelings of isolation tempt us to believe that we are alone. Orphaned. Putting on our "Can Do" attitude, we start looking in the world for solutions to make ourselves feel better. We don't want to hurt any more. We make the mistake of believing that following the rules and doing all the right things should insulate us from what is common to man. I believe Paul writes Romans 8:35 so that we understand that our adoption into the family of God does not shield us from trouble, hardship, persecution, or famine, or nakedness, or danger, or sword, or death.

In Galatians 3:2 Paul asks us, "Did you receive the Spirit by works of the law, or by believing what you heard?" Either we work hard under the law or believe in God's work through Jesus Christ to adopt us. Resting in this adoption is like resting in a recliner. Our adoption upholds and comforts us. We sit in it, get comfortable, put our feet up. We know that adoption is not dependent on the orphan, but the orphan is completely dependent on the one who adopts her. It is the same with our Heavenly Father.

Now that we know God, we know that we cannot earn a place in His family. We don't want to become slaves again thinking that we need to observe special days or follow special laws or man-made traditions to keep from experiencing the troubles that are common to all of humanity. We are the children of the free woman, and like Isaac we are children of promise (Galatians 4:9-10).

Whatever we are facing today, know that it cannot change our adoption into the family of God. When we face troubling times, we are tempted to think that others who appear more righteous on the outside have it easier, but the truth is that they fail to keep the laws they set up to make them feel more righteous. Most of the time rule followers are the most miserable. They are good at hiding

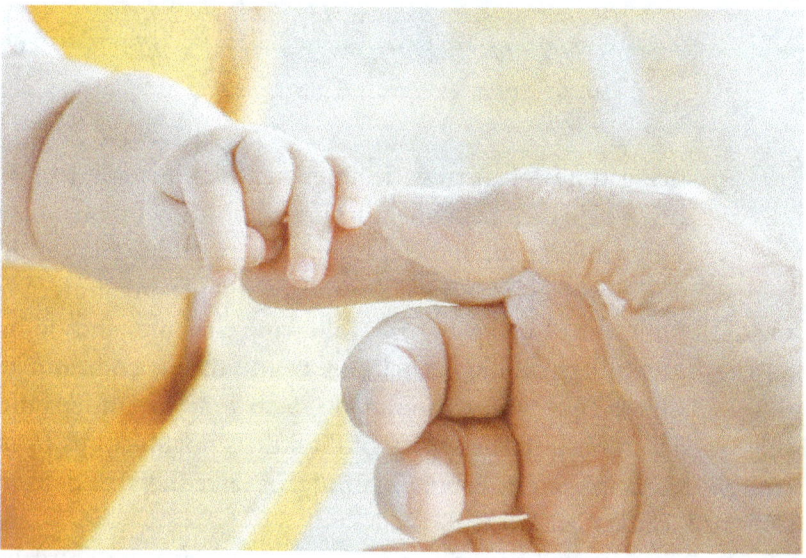

behind their mask of self-righteousness. Legalism keeps them from experiencing grace and love. For the legalist every bad thing that happens is condemnation. There is no love in this system.

We can't work harder to be more adopted. Either we believe in the Lord Jesus or we believe we are righteous by keeping the law. Jesus invites us to sit down into his work on the cross and be held by his Spirit that lives in our hearts, whereby we call out "Abba, Father." Some of the most beautiful words written are, "Who shall separate us from the love of God? Shall trouble, hardship, persecution, or famine, or nakedness, or danger, or sword?" Nothing can separate us from the love of God that is in Christ Jesus our Lord. We have been adopted and nothing can separate us from our Father.

Rest in adoption today, knowing that whatever you face, you face it with the Spirit in your heart that is even now interceding for you.

Day 6

Rest in Renewal

That, however, is not the way of life you learned when you heard about Christ and were taught in him in accordance with the truth that is in Jesus. You were taught, with regard to your former way of life, to put off your old self, which is being corrupted by its deceitful desires to be made new in the attitude of your minds and to put on the new self, created to be like God in true righteousness and holiness.
Ephesians 4:20-24

Resting in renewal is knowing that the attitude of our minds is being renewed. We once lived for ourselves. Now we live for God. Resting does not always mean inaction. Rest also means to refresh oneself or to recover strength. After knee surgery, the doctor sends us to rehab to recover our strength. Rehab is the opposite of inaction. We cannot recover from our former way of life by continuing to live in it. Just like the body works hard to repair and recover after surgery, God repairs and strengthens the soul.

Visually, in these verses I see myself taking off the coat of the old way of life and putting on the new coat of Christ. We can't take something off until we first identify what needs to be removed. "Deceitful desires" is a broad term that encompasses many attitudes, but Paul clarifies that we can be *deceived* by these desires. We have to ask ourselves, "What desires am I allowing to direct my life? What am I chasing after? What do I believe will bring me the most joy? If I can get this one thing, then I will be happy." That one thing is our god. It's what we allow to direct our lives. We depend on it for joy and fulfillment. Everyone who comes to faith in Christ must wrestle with these questions.

My biggest weak spots are approval, acceptance, and affirmation. I must diligently watch my motives for service because if I'm not careful, I find myself slipping my arms into that old coat of desire.

Just like rehab is specific to rebuild strength in the areas that are weakened, so we must be specific about the old coats that we need to take off, and then we diligently put on the new self. This process takes time. If we are not careful, we will give up. It can be overwhelming if we tried to do everything at one time. Start with asking God to open your eyes to the area where He is working.

*If we rest in the truth that we are being renewed,
we know that we can put on the new self
because we are created to be like God in true
righteousness and holiness.*

Day 7

Rest in the Knowledge of God

And this is my prayer: that your love may abound more and more in knowledge and depth of insight, so that you may be able to discern what is best and may be pure and blameless for the day of Christ, filled with the fruit of righteousness that comes through Jesus Christ- to the glory and praise of God. Philippians 1:9-11

The more I grow as a follower of Christ and experience times of deep distress, I find that I grow in my knowledge of God. To say that Job experienced deep distress is in an understatement. Until my son died, I didn't fully connect with the death of his ten children. Sadly, they were just a part of the list of everything he lost.

The Bible records that Job was a righteous man, so we know that he followed the law diligently. As his friends contended with him in his grief, Job answered, "Oh, that I had someone to hear me! I sign now my defense- let the Almighty answer me; let my accuser put his indictment in writing." Big words for a created being to the Uncreated One.

And the Holy, Uncreated One answered, "Who has a claim against me that I must pay? Everything under heaven belongs to me." After God finishes his questioning of Job, Job answers, "My ears had heard of you, but now my eyes have seen you." In other words, Job says, "I had heard of you, but now I know you." Through many hardships, Job moved from knowing God's promises and truths to experiencing them.

So often we make God like His creation because we can only know what is revealed. As I have suffered the common sufferings of man, I, all the more, sit in wonder that God revealed himself to us through Jesus Christ.

Resting in the knowledge of the Holy One is growing to know Him more. Hardship gives us the opportunity to take what we know and put it into action. We are made in His image, so we can love. God IS love. We behave in a loving manner, but God's very being is love. His essence is love.

Rest today knowing that He wants you to know and love Him more and more. If you are not where you want to be, He will continue to show Himself to you, so that you can be pure and blameless on the day of Christ. We always have room to grow in our knowledge of God. He is Incomprehensible after all! Take heart my friend, God is even now revealing Himself to you through His Word and the Spirit!

Day 8

Rest in Joy

Consider it pure joy, my brothers and sisters, whenever you face trials of many kinds, because you know that the testing of your faith produces perseverance. James 1:2

If we want to walk in faith, we must accept many, seemingly, opposing truths. Joy and trials create very different feelings in us. With trials come rejection, sadness, persecution, loss, etc., and we are to consider or count our trial as joy.

Romans 12:12 brings some clarification, "Be joyful in hope, patient in affliction, faithful in prayer." After my son died, a well-meaning friend asked, if I was happy that my son died. No. Who can honestly ever say that she is happy to endure the death of her child?

My joy is my hope. My hope is in Christ. Christ is my joy!

James says to consider or to think carefully about our trials. We can be joyful that the testing of our faith will produce perseverance and perseverance will finish its work so that we may be mature and complete, not lacking anything.

Both the righteous and the unrighteous encounter affliction. Repeat that with me, *BOTH the righteous and unrighteous must endure affliction.* We don't love affliction. Let's be honest; who can? Our joy is in what the affliction will produce in us. We will grow in our faith. Our hope in Christ will be made firm. As we persevere we will mature. Everyone wants to be complete, no one wants to be afflicted.

Most of us run after motivational speakers that make us feel good and tell us that God wants us to be satisfied in this life. Jesus doesn't model this for us. Isaiah wrote that he was a man of suffering and familiar with pain. He was oppressed and afflicted. Jesus said in John 13:16 "Very truly I tell you, no servant is greater than his master, nor is a messenger greater than the one who sent him."

In the darkness, we lose sight of these truths. Slowly, we can lose hope because our hope was in God satisfying our earthly desires. I had to come out of denial and deal with my misplaced hope. Affliction has a way of exposing our wrong beliefs and broken places. We can get bitter about it, or we can know that God loves us and want us to experience freedom from misplaced hope. He wants our freedom, and if allowing affliction frees us, then He allows affliction.

> *Resting in Joy means that we find our joy in Christ, knowing that we will be mature and complete, and we patiently wait in affliction, accepting that affliction will bring us freedom.*

Day 9

Rest in the Holy Spirit's Intercession

In the same way, the Spirit helps us in our weakness. We do not know what we ought to pray for, but the Spirit himself intercedes for us though wordless groans. And he who searches our hearts knows the mind of the Spirit, because the Spirit intercedes for God's people in accordance with the will of God... Who then is the one who condemns? No one. Christ Jesus who died—more than that, who was raised to life—is at the right hand of God and is also interceding for us.
Romans 8:26,27,34

Paul writes the word intercedes three times! He wants us to know that the Holy Spirit and Jesus are right now *intervening* on our behalf. They pray that the *will of God will be accomplished in our lives.*

When we experience affliction, we point our finger at God and accuse Him of afflicting us. This must be His will. I've been there. If God is infinite and powerful then why didn't he stop it. You can fill the "it" in with whatever your difficulty is. As followers of Christ, we must be able to give the answer to ourselves and others, who are hurting. Why does God allow affliction?

The problem is sometimes we don't want to accept the answer. God has a plan that He began before He laid the foundations of the earth. He allowed us to choose to depend on Him, or depend on ourselves. We would do the same thing as Eve. We want to be like God. We want to be our own god with our own plans. Now all of creation is broken.

God allowed us to choose. We choose sin, and sin causes all kinds of affliction. Some of us are feeling the effects of abuse, disease, infertility, miscarriages, etc. that our parents and grandparents passed down to us. We come up with different plans to save ourselves and think God should get on board. We simply want God to step in and keep us from affliction. But that is not His plan.

God's plan was to send Jesus, and through Jesus, God reconciled the world to Himself. Then Jesus went to heaven, and gave us the job to continue to the ministry of reconciliation. He's made known to us that the purpose of Christ is to bring unity to all things in heaven and on earth under Christ. Until the times reach their fulfillment His plan is for us to depend on Him.

> *We must find our rest in the Spirit and Jesus interceding for us that the will of God will be accomplished in our lives. We are not alone. We don't have to figure it out. We rest in intercession.*

Day 10

Rest in Repentance

*"...In repentance and rest is your salvation,
in quietness and trust is your strength..."*
Isaiah 30:15

Repentance is not a onetime event.
    1 John 1:8-10 "If we claim to be without sin, we deceive ourselves and the truth is not in us. If we confess our sins, he is faithful and just and will forgive us our sins and purify us from all unrighteousness. If we claim we have not sinned, we make him out to be a liar and his word is not in us."

Remember how rest has a few definitions? Rest means to recover strength, and it also means to refresh oneself.

John doesn't argue whether or not we sin. He says that if we claim we don't sin the truth is not in us. He takes the pressure of being perfect off our shoulders. We can unashamedly bow and repent. We need a change in perspective of repentance from negative to a time of refreshing.

Repentance is the only no-shame way to refresh our souls from sin. Any other way involves more sin. In repentance, we say that

God is bigger than us. His ways are right, and our ways are wrong. Bringing our sin into the Light frees us from bondage. We have nothing to hide from God.

As we learn to continually refresh our souls through repentance, we keep in focus what it cost our Savior. Through repentance we take the weight of our sin off our shoulders and place it on Jesus's. For this thing I've done, said, or thought, Jesus bled and died. For my freedom, he was raised to a new life. In this new life with Christ, we experience the comfort of the Holy Spirit. In John 14, Jesus tells His disciples that He will go away so that the Holy Spirit can come and live with us and will be in us. Repentance opens our heart to receive this comfort from the Holy Spirit.

You have heard that God is for you. It's an encouraging platitude that can keep us living in pride. James 4: 6 says, "God opposes the proud but gives grace to the humble." If we are proud and refuse to repent, then God opposes us. The Greek word means that He resists us like a football player stiff arming the coming opponent. God is for you because He made a way for you to repent. He wants all men to come to repentance (2 Peter 3:9).

When we repent, it can feel like death. As we refresh ourselves in repentance whatever is proud will die, and we will be made alive in Christ. As we moment by moment learn to rest in repentance, we will find that humbling ourselves grows easier as we see the fullness of God's love for us in Jesus our Savior.

Day 11

Rest in God's Faithfulness

*He is the Rock, His works are perfect, and
all his ways are just. A faithful God who does no
wrong, upright and just is he.*
Deuteronomy 32:4

The prophets of old longed to see the fruition of God's plan of salvation in Jesus. We have the joy and pleasure to see His unfolded plan. The enmity between the Serpent and Eve that began in the garden, "he will crush your head and you will strike his heel," came to an end on the Cross. God is faithful! Every prophecy of the coming Messiah found in the Old Testament was completed in Jesus Christ.

Why do we question His promises now? Because of affliction? What holds us back from resting in His faithfulness? God was faithful to generation after generation of Israelites. Historically, we know that what He spoke through the prophet Jeremiah and others came true. When the Israelites turned from God and began to worship foreign gods, God pursued His rebellious children through the prophets, but they continued to seek their own way. God allowed the Babylonians to crush the Israelites and carry off their young men. Later, Artaxerxes granted Nehemiah permission to rebuild Jerusalem, gave him letters for safe passage, and letters to acquire materials to rebuild. God's faithfulness is in the history books!

If God was faithful to the Israelites in their unfaithfulness, why would He change His promises to us? I ask again, knowing the affliction of the Israelites did not change God's promises, why would it change ours? We can be confident that He who began a good work in us will carry it on to completion until the day of Jesus Christ (Philippians 1:6). If God can save our souls, He will be faithful to meet any need we have.

There will be times that the way before us is dark and treacherous, but for His name sake He will guide us along the right paths. Even though we walk through the darkest valley, we will fear no evil because God is faithful (Psalm 23).

Sometimes when our way is dark and filled with pain, we can become afraid. God never promised us that this life will be free of pain, struggle, hardship, or loss. If we misunderstand the promise of God's salvation as mainly displayed through this physical world and our comfort, then fear and misunderstanding will lead us to question God's faithfulness. When what is common to man assails us, we will doubt God. He promises to give us everything we need for life and godliness. He's given us a divine nature. Through Him we escape the corruption of the world caused by evil desires (Hebrews 1:3-4). We have many great promises. As we learn to rest in God's faithfulness we guard our hearts from unbelief and fear in a corrupt world.

Let us rest in God's faithfulness! He has never failed to fulfill a promise and He's not going to stop being who He is.

God is faithful! Nothing that we face today can change His faithfulness.

Day 12
Rest in a New Citizenship

But our citizenship is in heaven. And we eagerly await a Savior from there, the Lord Jesus Christ, who, by the power that enables him to bring everything under his control, will transform our lowly bodies so that they will be like his glorious body.
Philippians 3:20-21

This world is not my home.

The more I face affliction, the more I hear of tragedies, the more I long for my heavenly home. The older I get and the more my body changes, the more I long for my heavenly body. Let's face it — getting old is not for the faint of heart!

The brokenness of this world and the devastation of sin breaks our hearts daily. We long for the Savior to ride in on

a white horse, whose rider is called Faithful and True. With justice he judges and wages war. His eyes are like blazing fire and on his head, are

*many crowns. He is dressed in a robe dipped in
blood, and his name is the Word of God… On
his robe and on his thigh,
he has this name written:*

*"King of Kings and Lord of Lords."
Revelation 19:11-16*

Let us not be distracted by the world and its pleasures. We belong to King of Kings and Lord of Lords. We easily fall back into the distractions of this world. What will we eat and what will we wear? In Matthew 6 Jesus says, "Do not store up for yourselves treasures on earth, where moths and vermin destroy and where thieves break in and steal. But store up for yourselves treasures in heaven…For where your treasure is there you heart will be also."

If our home is in heaven, then let us rest in our heavenly citizenship. The worries and afflictions in this life can be overwhelming. Our hearts break and we say, "it's not supposed to be this way." May these very words remind us that there is coming a day that Jesus will set everything right. Until then remember this ...

"(God), You keep track of all my sorrows. You have collected all my tears in your bottle. You have recorded each one in your book." Psalm 56:8. God knows our sorrows! Know that when we enter our heavenly home God, "will wipe away every tear from their eyes. There will be no more death or mourning or crying, or pain, for the old order of things has passed away," Revelation 21:4

*Learning to rest in our heavenly citizenship gives
us hope even as the evil of this world grieves us.*

Day 13
Rest in Grace

You then, my son, be strong in the grace that is in Christ Jesus. 2 Timothy 2:1

The gifts of grace are never ceasing and overflowing beyond measure. This gift is not like the trespass. Judgement for sin followed one sin and brought condemnation, but the gift followed many trespasses and brought justification. If death came though one man, how much more will those who receive God's abundant provision of grace and the gift of righteousness reign in life through the one-man Jesus Christ! (Romans 5).

Resting in grace is relinquishing our plans and ways. We are always calculating. We got sums and totals in our heads. If I do this, then that will happen. The difficulty is that we cannot draw a straight line from our actions to our blessings. When we can't manipulate the people and situations in our lives to get the desired outcome that we want and when we try, we are left frustrated and angry, feeling like we have been robbed. We condemn ourselves to feeling that we are not enough. Simply, we rob ourselves of our freedom in Christ, when we try to convince ourselves that we are enough.

Humbling ourselves in grace is admitting that we aren't enough. Everything about coming to faith in Jesus Christ is about admitting that we are not enough. We are not righteous enough for salvation. We need a Messiah. We cannot live the Christian life in our flesh. We must walk in the Spirit. We can do nothing on our own. We must humble ourselves to God's ways and abandon the fruitless ways of humanity that is handed down generation after generation.

God didn't design us to be enough. He designed us to need Him and want Him and worship Him. Anything less than God, we fall from grace and are alienated from Christ. Therefore, whatever we use to make ourselves enough is an idol and a lie.

Sometimes these idols are good things or ways that we have used to cope with affliction in this life. We make idols out of marriage, work, money, motherhood, Christian service, success etc. We put our faith in many things. A great difficulty for the Christian is to acknowledge a lie that she has believed.

When tragedy threatens our idols, we make the mistake of believing that God doesn't love us. However, in His great love for us, He is tearing down for us what enslaves us. Does it hurt? Yes. Will you grieve? Yes. God's grace frees us from the lies we tell ourselves and the idols that enslave us.

> *Today let us rest in the boundless grace of God*
> *that we did not earn and couldn't have planned.*
> *We didn't even know we needed Jesus until he*
> *came to us.*

Day 14
Rest in Truth

Guide me in your truth and teach me, for you are God my Savior, and my hope is in you all day long. Psalm 25:5

While reading Francis Chan's book, *Erasing Hell*, I came across his prayer, "God, prevent my desire to twist scripture to gratify my personal preferences." We are all tempted to do this. We all have habits, hurts, and hang-ups, and as we read scripture, we have the best intentions to find healing for our brokenness, but our feelings, wants, heartaches, and desires are not ultimate. Only God is ultimate.

We live in a postmodern world. Even the word postmodern is difficult to define because to define it would violate the postmodernist's premise that no definite terms, boundaries, or absolute truths exist. Because of our wants and desires as Christians sometimes we are conformed to our culture, rather than being transformed by the renewing of our minds (Romans 12:2). We deceive ourselves with our best intentions. We conform to the culture that casts off boundaries and truth in favor of defining themselves. Resting in truth requires us to allow the Word of God to define right and wrong. God's Truth defines even our identity.

Jesus answered, "I am the way and the truth and the life. No one comes to the Father except through me" (John 14:6). We must pray daily to be guided by God's truth. Watching our lives carefully, so that we don't disqualify ourselves!

> *"So, if you think you are standing firm, be*
> *careful that you don't fall!"*
> 1 Corinthians 10:12

This is a good word for us to keep in mind as we walk through life, whether we are enduring affliction or we are rejoicing. Let's be aware of our needs and desires, so that we can be guided to truth and taught by our Savior. It's so easy to be misguided by our feelings, wants, heartaches, and desires. Because, let's be honest, most of our desires are deeply needed. We all need to be loved and to find approval, acceptance. We have needs, but our needs are not ultimate.

Also, we must understand the deceptive nature of sin. We don't know we are being deceived until the truth is revealed. Because of the deceitfulness of sin, we should live in relationship with other believers who can encourage us daily. They can see what we cannot. Find a trusted friend who will challenge you to see where your desires and feelings are not lining up with God's truth.

> *Today let's rest in Truth!*
> *God's Word is Truth!*

Day 15

Rest in Endurance

As you know, we count as blessed those who have persevered. You have heard of Job's perseverance and have seen what the Lord finally brought about. The Lord is full of compassion and mercy. James 5:11

Rest and endurance seem opposed to one another. In the summer of 2017, my husband and I started running. Like any good students would do, we got a book, *Galloway's Book on Running* by Jeff Galloway. His method of running is unique in that it combines intervals of intense running with walking recovery. Perusing his table of contents, you see chapter titles like: Getting Started, Planning, Speed, and most important, Pacing!

Endurance is less about who gets there the fastest, and more about who finishes. Maybe you are like me, and you need a one to one ratio. Run for one minute, and then walking rest for one minute to recover. How does this translate to spiritual endurance?

James refers us to Job. His anxiety inducing story tempts us to skip from Job "is a righteous man" to "and God restored his fortunes and gave him back twice as much as he had before," missing all the middle messy parts. Job was rightfully depressed ripping his clothes and cursing the day of his birth. Remember all ten of his children died on the same day. He wanted to die! He wanted God to crush him. He wallowed in self-pity saying that he had become a laughing stock. But he endured to the end.

Like Job, Abraham's life exemplifies endurance. Yes, he believed God and it was credited to him for righteousness. But, he also tried to have a child on his own without God by using Sarah's servant, Hagar. The middle parts of his story get very messy as well. He even lies to protect himself while putting his wife in danger, but he endured to the end. When God tested him, Abraham said, "God himself will provide the lamb."

I don't want to even describe my messy middle of grief. It was ugly. All our middle parts can get messy because, although we know God, we can't know everything about Him. As we endure through many trials, we learn more of His being, His attributes, His character, and His acts. Like Job and Abraham, as our life becomes less about us and more about knowing God, we begin to rest in our relationship with Him. At first my faith was about fixing my problems, but after grief, I realized faith is more than fixing problems. Faith is knowing God. I still have problems, but I have grown to know God more deeply. When hardship rips our illusions of control from us, spiritual pacing reminds us that it's ok to slow down. It's ok to grieve, feel the loss. It's ok to be sad for a time. I've learned that God neither pushes or pulls us through it. He walks by our side. God, our Father, is in control, and we can learn to enjoy Him as we walk together through it. We echo Abraham's wise words, "God himself will provide."

Learning to rest in endurance acknowledges that sometimes we walk instead of run. We need more quiet moments in prayer than many actions. We rest in the power of God to endure difficulty without giving way. Maybe yesterday we struggled to believe, but today we will say, "God himself will provide."

Day 16

Rest in the Torn Veil

It was now about noon, and darkness came over the whole land until three in the afternoon for the sun stopped shining. And the curtain of the temple was torn in two. Jesus called out with a loud voice, "Father, into your hands I commit spirit." When he had said this, he breathed his last. Luke 23:44-46

To fully understand the significance of the torn curtain, we must go back to the Old Testament and the Temple. The curtain separated the Holy Place from the Most Holy Place, where the ark of the covenant was kept. No one could enter the Most Holy Place without dying, except the High Priest. That was permitted only once a year after a ceremonial cleansing. The High Priest would tie a rope around his waist. In the event that he did something wrong and died as a result, they could drag him out from behind the curtain. The curtain represents our separation from God and His protection for sinners. The size of this great curtain was so awesome that it prevented one from accidently falling into the Most Holy Place. It took 300 priests to move it.

The curtain protects sinful man from the wrath of a Holy God. We cannot come to God by our plans or desires. We can come to God only through Jesus.

While on the cross, Jesus' mangled body hung, His own body was given as payment for our sins and His death satisfied the wrath of God. What was due to us, He took because He paid a debt He did not owe for a debt we could never pay.

At the very moment that "Jesus cried out again with a loud voice and yielded up his spirit" (Matthew 27:50) "the curtain of the temple was torn in two, from top to bottom. And the earth shook, and the rocks were split" (Matthew 27:51). The curtain was torn at the exact moment of Jesus's death because we no longer needed it's protection or separation. Notice that the temple curtain was torn from the top down to the bottom indicating that it was torn by God Himself. What no human could possible tear by human strength, God did by the death of the Son of God. Now we can go behind the curtain and have access into the Most Holy Place.

Let us rest because the torn curtain symbolizes our access to God. Now "we have confidence to enter the holy places by the blood of Jesus" (Hebrews 10:19).

Although, distress causes us to feel like we have no options, nowhere to run, or to hide, the torn veil begs us into the presence of the Father. He has made Himself the hiding place. Learning to rest in this truth brings comfort to our souls during affliction. We have a place to rest.

Day 17

Rest in God's Blessings

The Beatitudes
Matthew 5:3-12

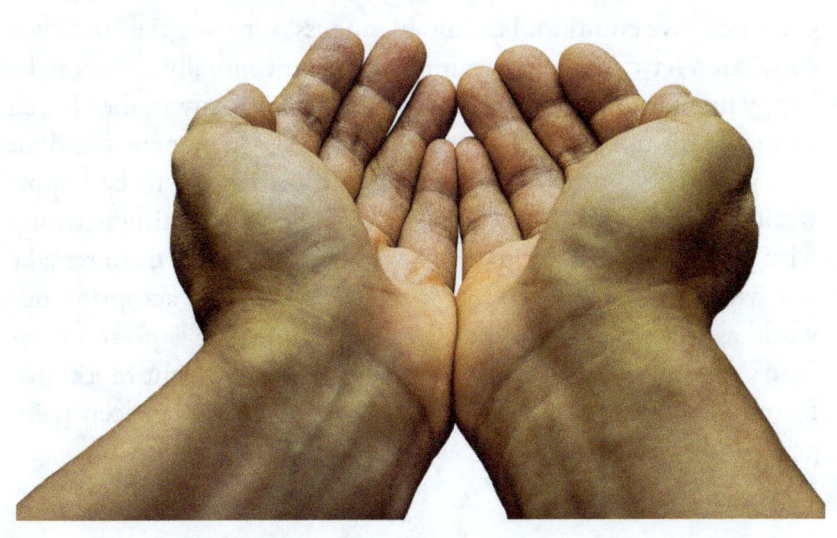

God does not give as the world gives. He doesn't see blessings the way we see blessings. God gives good gifts to the righteous and the unrighteous, to those who love Him and to those who are far away.

"Blessed are those who mourn, because they will be comforted" Matthew 5:4.

In the deepest parts of my grief, I hated this verse because I felt anything but blessed. Perhaps you too have had times of overwhelming pain from whatever storm you are facing. During my storm of grief, a few ladies sought to comfort me by saying "push through" and "just get over it." At first, I was deeply hurt. How does one get over a loss such as mine? Then I considered their lives. Each had been deeply hurt by their dads. They learned to insulate themselves from the pain by numbing their feelings and wearing a mask that said, "I'm good. I'm happy. Nothing's wrong with me." They didn't know how to mourn, and that's when this verse made sense. Being able to mourn is a blessing because then you will receive comfort.

Our culture embraces what Susan David calls false positivity. (https://www.ted.com/talks/susan_david_the_gift_and_power_of_emotional_courage/transcript) This is when we avoid and dismiss every negative emotion. Feelings of sadness, sorrow, grief, and even conviction have no place in our lives. It is now morally correct to be happy no matter the situation. Unfortunately, many in the church embrace this mask of false positivity as well. This opens the door to a prosperity gospel which says, "God wants you to be happy, wealthy, and healthy," and if you're not, then something is wrong with your faith. The desire to always be happy forces us to remake our world into what we want it to be, rather than accepting our world as it is. In the world of false positivity there is no room for God's discipline or for us to be used to shine the light of a transforming, redeeming gospel because they often bring deep pain, grief, and conviction.

In the Beatitudes, Jesus upends human wisdom and false positivity. He calls us to a whole new way to live. By nature, our minds resist disharmony and pain. Although we want only happiness and good things, that is not the way the righteous are able to live in a corrupt world. Jesus says we are blessed when we are poor in spirit, when we mourn, when we are gentle, hungry, and merciful. We are blessed when we are pure in heart, make peace, and are persecuted and insulted. As we embrace this truth, we learn to rest in God's blessing. We don't have to put on a shiny happy face. As Christians we are called to mourn with those who mourn (Romans 12:15).

No matter what we face, we rest in God's blessings that are incorruptible and unperishable. Though we grieve, we know that we will be comforted. If we show mercy, we will be shown mercy. When we are insulted or persecuted, we are blessed!

Day 18

Rest in God's Pursuit of Sinners

Even if you have banished me to the most distant land under heavens, from there the Lord your God will gather you and bring you back.
Deuteronomy 30:4

Jesus stood up in the assembly and read, "The Spirit of the Lord is on me, because he has anointed me to proclaim good news to the poor. He has sent me to proclaim freedom for the prisoners and recovery of sight for the blind to set the oppressed free to proclaim the year of the Lord's favor." Luke 4:18-19.

Sometimes I sit here in this truth and meditate. Jesus was anointed to proclaim good news to the poor. He was sent to free the captives. Sin holds every soul captive. God sent Jesus running to meet us. Freedom for prisoners…

The story of the prodigal son fascinates me (Luke 15:11-32). Here, this son dishonors his father by grabbing his inheritance.

He can't even wait for his father to die. He runs and spends all his father's hard-earned money on "wild living." Can you imagine? Working year after year, toiling away, saving, and sacrificing and in a short time your son has spent all your money on unrighteous living. I'm not ashamed to say that I would be angry as I think about it. I'm not God.

God is fundamentally not like us. He is not like our earthly parents, who although may have done the best they could, failed us in many ways. God loves His creation. He declared it very good. He wants us. He pursues sinners.

Answer this question: Is God like earthly fathers? Don't give the Sunday School answer. What do you really think?

The Father went to the road to see if he could see his son coming home. The Father doesn't wait for the son to get close. No, *no, no, no, no,* while the son is a long way off, the Father runs to him and throws his arms around the son. He throws a party, bringing all his best food, and puts his robe on the son and a ring for his finger. All the son wanted was to be a servant in his father's house, but instead he was restored and celebrated. What was lost is now found!

Let me tell you I spent way too many years thinking that I "got one" over on God. 2 Peter says, "(he) is patient not wanting any to perish, but all to come to repentance."

I didn't think I was good enough for friendship with Christ. I thought I "got one over" on God because His word said "all" and "any." Because I was "any" and "all," He *had* to forgive me. I wanted to be a servant in the house of the Lord. What I found was that God *had* me. He pursued me. He calls us to not only be servants, but He calls us First Born sons and daughters!

> *Rest in God's pursuit of you!* He loves you and wants you to be His child. He has thrown His arms around you and clothed you in His best garment, Jesus Christ!

Day 19

Rest in God's Mercy

*He saved us, not because of the righteous
things we have done, but because of His mercy.
He saved us through the washing of rebirth and
renewal by the Holy Spirit, whom he poured out
on us generously through Jesus Christ our Savior.*
Titus 3:5

The simplicity of the gospel is what makes it so appealing. We don't have to be told that we are sinners. We are really good at being selfish by the age of two.

Resting in God's mercy should be straight forward, but it's not. Paul wrote a letter to the Galatians because like us they struggled with this very thing. The Galatians had been taught the truth by Paul himself. The main controversy was over circumcision. Although we don't struggle with circumcision, we do struggle with trying to live by the old code of the law to earn God's approval.

In our brokenness from various storms, we forget the mercy of God. Galatians 3:2 "Did you receive the Spirit by the works of the law, or by believing what you heard?"

None of us are worthy enough to gain God's approval by our goodness or good works. Let's not fall back into the old ways of the law in the storm.

Maybe at this point you are wondering why the law was even given. Paul answers, "I would not have known what sin was had it not been for the law. For I would not have known what coveting really was if the law had not said, 'You shall not covet' (Romans 7:7)."

The law was given so we would know we are sinners, not to make us righteous. How can we now be righteous by obeying the law or doing good works? The storms of life happen to everyone, the righteous and unrighteous.

By faith we accept Jesus as Lord and Savior. Let us not run back to slavery in times of trouble. Let us hold on to Hebrews 4:16, "Let us then approach God's throne of grace with confidence, so that we may receive mercy and find grace to help us in our time of need."

Slavery takes the form of many different masks we try to hide behind. Some of us, like the Pharisees, cling to our righteousness and family heritage. Some of us exhaust ourselves trying to be good enough. We hide behind our good works. Galatians 3:26-27 says, "So in Christ Jesus you are all children of God through faith, for all of you who were baptized into Christ have clothed yourselves with Christ." God's mercy frees us from the slavery of earning our own righteousness. We don't need the right family heritage. We can cease trying to be good enough. God clothed us with Christ. We can rest in His mercy free from every mask we've ever worn.

And, let 1 Peter 1:3-4 comfort us, "Praise be to the God and Father of our Lord Jesus Christ! In his great mercy he has given us new birth into a living home through the resurrection of Jesus Christ from the dead and into an inheritance that can never perish spoil or fade. This inheritance is kept in heaven for you."

Today we rest in His mercy because our hope is Jesus Christ, and our inheritance is in heaven, where it can never spoil or fade.

Day 20

Rest in the Process of Being Made Holy

… (we) are being transformed into his image with ever increasing glory, which comes from the Lord, who is Spirit.
2 Corinthians 3:18

Being transformed is a process. If we are lucky enough to be born, we are born to broken parents. We went to school with broken friends and broken teachers. We grow up to have broken co-workers and broken bosses. We have broken spouses. Our world influences us. The way we react can be rooted in our hurts, habits, and hang-ups. I don't know about you, but whatever I'm doing, I like to get done, quickly. If I could talk to my younger self, the first thing I would say is, "SLOW DOWN."

I don't want to hurt. I don't want to keep failing. I want to be perfect as my Heavenly Father is perfect, and I want it right now!

Sanctification is the process of being made holy. There are steps of discipleship that must take place. Sometimes we can skip steps, but it's not likely. Our faith must be tested. Testing and trials don't always feel good. But, it's not about feeling good, it's about being made into the image of Christ. Romans 8:18, "I consider that our present sufferings are not worth comparing with the glory that will be revealed in us."

When we rest in the process of being made holy, we consider. Consider means to think carefully about (something), typically before deciding. Our first gut reaction is to hurt, lament, feel any range of emotion, and *then we think*. We can't always control our emotions, but we can change our thoughts. By taking time to carefully think about our tests and trials, we can take the next step to compare them to the future glory that will be revealed in us. This process can take time as we "demolish arguments and every pretention that sets itself up against the knowledge of God and take captive every thought to make it obedient in Christ," (2 Corinthians 10:5).

This doesn't sound like rest, meaning inactivity, but we rest in the knowledge that it is a process. I can think of several occasions that I had to forgive someone. In those situations, God tested me. My first reaction was fear because I couldn't do it. I hurt too much, but as I humbled myself, God showed me the many places He repeatedly forgives me. When I think about Jesus on the cross bearing the weight and punishment of my sins, it makes me consider. If Jesus would do that for me, I can let go of my feelings that someone is in my debt. Forgiveness takes one person. Forgiveness is not reconciliation. Because we forgive we are forgiven. Reconciling friendly relations with the person who hurt us takes both parties working together, and sometimes we don't get that.

Today, rest in the process of being made holy.
Be assured that God is even now at work
transforming you!

Day 21

Rest in the Beauty of Christ

"… but woman is man's glory."
1 Corinthians 11:7

What do women really need? Do they need to hear they are beautiful? Does this really heal their broken self-image? For a moment, and then tomorrow we will need to hear it again because believing we are beautiful does not heal our broken self-image. It puts a salve on it. It soothes the pain that sin has caused, but it doesn't take it away.

Our self-image was forever broken in the garden, when Eve questioned God's goodness and His plan for her. She saw that the fruit looked good. Sin always looks good, and then it turns on you. She wanted to know for herself. She didn't want to trust God. She wanted to determine what is good for herself. From the moment she ate the fruit, she knew she was naked, and now our cravings and desires will sway and distort our ability to reason. We have the cloud of sin, a broken self-image. We cannot see ourselves as we truly are, and often, those who sin against us blame our beauty for their cravings.

And here is the problem. How does God fix it? I can look in the mirror and recite mantra after mantra, "I am beautiful." I may feel better, a little, but my self-image is broken. This mantra, "You are beautiful!" fails to restore our self-image. Only Jesus gives us Truth in a world filled with lies.

I can never be good enough, kind enough, or pretty enough. I still fail. I still fail to do all that I want to do. Even my best is not enough. Isaiah 64:6 says, "All of us have become like one who is unclean, and all our righteous acts are like filthy rags; we all shrivel up like a leaf, and like the wind our sins sweep us away." I must take responsibility for the sin in my life that has broken my self-image. So, how can we truly be beautiful?

Romans 13:14 says, "Rather, clothe yourselves with the Lord Jesus Christ, and do not think about how to gratify the desires of the flesh." How does this happen? 2 Corinthians 5:21 says, "God made him who had no sin to be sin for us, so that in him we might become the righteousness of God." His righteousness and clean garments are ours by faith. They become ours at the moment of our salvation.

Resting in the beauty of Christ is knowing that with our first step of faith we begin a life-long journey of growing in our knowledge of Christ. Knowing Jesus is the goal of our salvation.

In Him, I am completely beautiful. He gave me His beauty! I can rest in His beauty!

Day 22

Rest in the Righteousness of Christ

God made him who had no sin to be sin for us, so that in him we might become the righteousness of God. 2 Corinthians 5:21

Certain platitudes said to me by well-meaning Christian women to comfort me during a time of affliction concerns me. Maybe you have heard it lately too.

"You are worthy!"

A great chasm exists between the words "worth" and "worthy." One of them I have (worth), and one of them, I am not (worthy). Although, the English language is not always precise, however, we unintentionally create heresy and added hardship for hurting people, when we confuse worth and worthy. The definition of worth is the value equivalent to that of someone or something under consideration; the level at which someone or something deserves to be valued or rated. We use worth as a noun.

What determines worth or value? Generally, what people are willing to pay for an item determines worth. The value of the human soul is determined by the God who created it. Our worth is inherent, unmerited, and untouchable. God has no favorites. Every soul is the same in His sight. God loves and values the prostitute on the street as much as the Queen of England in Buckingham Palace. Inherent in every soul is worth because God created them. I'll write it again. *Worth is intrinsic. Worth is unmerited. Worth is untouchable.*

Many good people with great intentions want to free us from the bondage of low self-esteem by adding a "y" to the end of the word *worth* saying, "You are worthy!" What is implied in this statement is "you deserve good things" or "you have earned something better." We unintentionally further the weight of bondage by telling hurting people they are worthy. I found myself asking, "If I am worthy of something better, then why is affliction tormenting me. Why have I been abused?"

Paul clarifies that none of us are worthy in Romans 3:10-12 "There is no one righteous, not even one: there is no one who understand; there is no one who seeks God. All have turned away. They have together become worthless; there is no one who does good, no not even one." This demonstrates that we have all sinned and so we cannot be worthy of God's salvation. Our behavior here is the issue, not our intrinsic worth.

> *Jesus came because we are unworthy on our own. If I am worthy apart from Jesus, then I don't need a Savior. Learning to rest in the righteousness of Jesus is knowing that God made him who had no sin to be sin for us, so that in him we might become the righteousness of God.*

Day 23

Rest in the Love of Christ

But God demonstrates his own love for us in this: While we were sinners, Christ died for us.
Romans 5:8

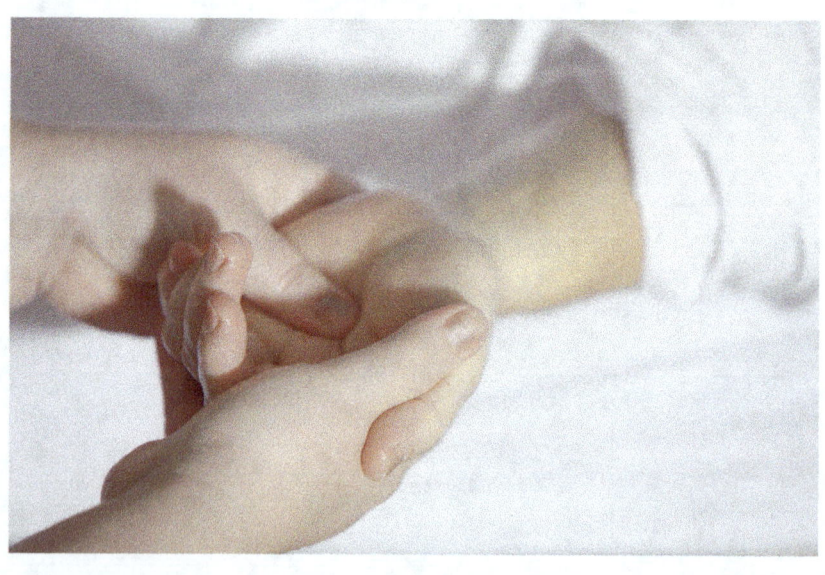

What beautiful words! God demonstrated His love. When my son died, I hurt so much I despaired, "Maybe God doesn't love me?" In my brokenness, I couldn't imagine God loving me and allowing me to hurt so much.

Maybe you are like me, and you struggle believing that Jesus loves you. Abuse and affliction steal our dignity and self-worth. Even the message we hear from the world is to be loved we must earn our place, prove our usefulness, and show our value. We have to work for it.

Sometimes, while in the storm, we ask for a sign of His love. In unbelief, we doubt His love and ask Him to demonstrate His love with an extra sign other than Christ on the cross. In my weakest hour I asked for a sign that God loved me. I'm thankful I asked for a rainbow because they are more rare than pink sunsets or hearing my favorite song on the radio. God denied me a rainbow. I am so thankful that He did.

In the storm, I cried out, "God, if you love me, then save me from this hurt." He whispered back, "I already have. I sent my Son. He humbled himself into the womb of a woman. He experienced every human struggle, and did not sin. He is your sign that I love you. He paid the debt for all your sin. He ripped the curtain that separated us. Let my rainbow be my promise to not flood the earth, and enjoy the pink sunsets that I created to declare my glory. Let Jesus be the sign of my love for you. I will always walk with you in hurt. Depend on me."

Every morning God whispers, "I love you! Look at Jesus and see how I love you." Romans 8: 32 says, "He who did not spare his own Son, but gave him up for us all—how will he not also, along with him, graciously give us all things?" These words sooth my aching soul in the storms of life.

Rest today knowing that God demonstrated His love for you through Jesus. We need no other sign. Enjoy the beauty of His creation, but let Jesus demonstrate His love for you! God walks with us through the storm, and nothing can separate us from His love
Romans 8:34-39.

Day 24

Day Rest in the Straight Path

*But small is the gate and narrow the
road that leads to life, and only a few find it.
Matthew 7:14*

This seems *straight forward*! Which way leads to life? The narrow road. Which way leads to destruction, the wide road. When the storms of life come, which way is easier? Jesus tells us that few find the narrow road. When I'm afraid of the storm, I want a friend with me, lots of friends.

The wide road looks so tempting. Everyone is there. It's popular and in style. I want to be liked. Who wants to be ostracized or forgotten? We all want to be important. We want to be insulated from the storm. Who knowingly walks right into a tornado?

I didn't even recognize I was walking right into a tornado, until my faith stopped making sense.

Before my son died, I didn't even recognize how the soft prosperity gospel blinded me and my circle of friends. It's influence is so subtle. I was blessed, so why is this tornado wrecking my life? We were losing everything: son, house, job, friends, and church. I faced the truth that God never promises to rescue us from the situations of earthly life that sin causes or the brokenness that follows. Whether that is our sin or someone else's sin against us.

We naturally gravitate towards teachers that inspire and make us feel good about ourselves. We want to be told that we are basically good. We are worthy and beautiful. We prefer a feel-good, self-empowerment gospel. We believe we have absolute authority to create our world through positive thinking and faith-based confessions. We've exchanged the God of the Bible for moralistic therapeutic deism that appeals to our desires.

Jesus teaches that His Kingdom is not of this world. To be first we must be the servant of all. The way that leads to destruction is broad. The road that leads to righteousness is straight and the gate is narrow. The righteous will be persecuted. Almost everything He teaches is the opposite of our natural inclinations, including suffering.

The rain falls on the just and the unjust, Matthew 5:45. All of us would like the right amount of rain at just the right time to fall for our greatest comfort. Some of us are poor, some of us have endured abuse, some of us are plagued by tragedy, and some of us have too many children, while others have none.

> *Resting in the straight path is learning to accept that God's ways are not our ways. He counts as blessed those whose sins are forgiven. As Reinhold Niebuhr writes in the Serenity Prayer, "accepting hardship as a pathway to peace; taking as Jesus did this sinful world as it is, not as I would have it, trusting that You will make all things right…"*

Rest in the truth that the gate is small and the path is narrow and few find it.

Day 25

Rest in the Peace of Christ

Therefore, since we have been justified through faith, we have peace with God through our Lord Jesus Christ, through whom we have gained access by faith into this grace in which we now stand. And we boast in the hope of the glory of God. Not only so, but we also glory in our sufferings, because we know that suffering produces perseverance. Romans 5:1-3

In this world we search for peace. We want a tangible peace that we can wrap our arms around or feel deeply without having to believe in something we can't see.

Before Jesus left His disciples, he said, "I am leaving you with a gift- peace of mind and heart. And the peace I give is a gift the world cannot give. So, don't be troubled or afraid." (John 14:27) In the storm, we see the darkness. We use the term darkness in so many ways, but as I faced storms in my life, the Lord reminded me that He created darkness too. Genesis records that "God made two great lights- the greater light to have dominion over the day and the lesser light to have dominion over the night- as well as the stars. God has authority over the darkness. I read somewhere once that there is nothing that can overtake you that God has not allowed.

Think of the night and the moon. Close your eyes and see God's created time for rest. Every day, He has ordained a time for us to lie down, release the cares of the day, and sleep, unafraid of the night. What if the very darkness we face is an ordained time for us to learn to rest in God? Would knowing that God still has authority over darkness, change how we Trust Him and experience His gift of peace? For me, the moon has become the physical reminder that God has dominion over my darkness.

Now remember that God *is* Light and there is no darkness in Him. We must believe this to experience victory in this life. None. There is no darkness in Him. He rules over the darkness, and "In Christ Jesus" you have victory over whatever you are facing. It's not a feeling, it's a truth you must believe.

Matthew records for us the ultimate scene of darkness, the Cross. At noon until three darkness covered the whole land. Then Jesus cries out, "My God, My God, why have You forsaken Me?"

Then some men offered Jesus some sour wine. Jesus shouted again with a loud voice and gave up His spirit.

Darkness. What amazing things was God, the Father, accomplishing in that darkness through Jesus, His Son? It looked like Satan might triumph. Jesus buried in a tomb. Don't forget that resurrection Sunday came, right on time!

> *Let us Rest in the Peace of Christ! He doesn't give as the world does. His peace makes us right before a Holy God, and He walked through the darkness to get it!*

Day 26

Rest in Adversity

Blessed are you when people insult you, persecute you and falsely say all kinds of evil against you because of me. Rejoice and be glad, because great is your reward in heaven, for in the same way they persecuted the prophets who were before you.   Matthew 5:11-12

I always thought insults, slander, and persecution would come from outside the church. My brothers and sisters in Christ would never insult me or persecute me. We would be able to meet and work out anything in the unity of Christ. Yes, I know; I was naive.

No one wants to think about wolves in the church, but both Jesus and Paul warn us about wolves. Sometimes wolves don't know they are wolves. Sometimes wolves are hurting people, weighed down by many sins, that have listened to false teaching. They don't mean to persecute those who speak truth. They want comfort, but they want comfort that appeals to their pleasures, wants, desires, and heartaches. They have a form of godliness, but deny its power (2 Timothy 3:1-9).

Resting in affliction doesn't sound fun, and it isn't. It's challenging like hiking through snow. We need the right equipment to guard against the cold and the right food to sustain us. Walking in snow is arduous, but the beauty is worth the work. Learning to rejoice in insults and persecution uses every definition of rest. We cease trying to be good enough to be accepted or approved. We strengthen spiritual muscles that are weak like forgiveness. We refresh our souls with *our* repentance. It does no good to remember other people's sins.

Ephesians 6:12 reminds us that "our struggle is not against flesh and blood, but against the rulers, against the authorities, against the powers of this dark world and against the spiritual forces of evil in the heavenly realms." We hurt deeply because insults are coming from the mouths of people we love. Learning to love them despite how they treat us flexes spiritual muscles to love like Christ does. He loved us, while we were sinners. We learn to refresh ourselves knowing that Jesus said this would happen. We hold onto these truths, when people in or outside the church insult, slander, or persecute us. I don't know the beauty that will come from our perseverance during these times. Jesus gives only this, "because great is your reward in heaven, for in the same way they persecuted the prophets who were before you."

> *Learning to rest in adversity is challenging, but we are promised great rewards in heaven. These truths will sustain you through the storm of persecution.*

Day 27

Rest in the Sufficiency of God

The God who made the world and everything in it is the Lord of heaven and earth and does not live in temples built by human hands. And he is not served by human hands, as if he needed anything. Rather, he himself gives everyone life and breath and everything else.
Acts 17:25

In our experience nothing is complete in itself. In elementary school we learn how to classify life. Everything alive has three basic needs: food, water, and air. We do a great disservice to ourselves when we forget the uniqueness of God. He is the only self-sufficient being.

A.W. Tozer writes in *The Knowledge of the Holy*, "Probably the hardest thought of all for our natural egotism to entertain is that God does not need our help. We commonly represent Him as a busy, eager, somewhat frustrated Father hurrying about seeking help to carry out His benevolent plan to bring peace and salvation to the world."

All that exists needs God. We learn to rest in God's sufficiency, when we stop trying to help Him fix our lives.

Acts 17:28, "For in him we live and move and have our being."

The greatest thing we can do is surrender to His way of salvation. Let us not throw off what is uniquely God and make Him like man. We need to be careful that we don't portray our God like Jolly Old St. Nicolas, a loving god who just doles out pleasure and grants desires. At times we are, as Tozer says, "divesting Him of His burning holiness and unapproachable majesty, the very attributes He veiled while on earth but assumed in fullness of glory upon His ascension to the Father's right hand."

In the storm we are tempted to believe God is hurrying around trying to figure out a way to save us. Following God becomes more about finding solutions to our problems, and less about being obedient to God. I read the other day this quote, "When we activate our faith, miracles happen." It may be an encouraging platitude, but God doesn't need our faith to be activated to work miracles. He is able to calm the storm without our faith (Luke 8:22-25). What He does ask is for us to be obedient.

Steps of obedience don't always make sense. Pray for my enemies (Matthew 5:44). Forgive others as God has forgiven me (Matthew 6:15).

> *Learning to rest in the sufficiency of God is knowing that He has everything under control even when it doesn't feel like it. His sufficiency should "lift the exhausting load of mortality and encourage us to take the easy yoke of Christ and spend ourselves in Spirit-inspired toil for the honor of God and the good of mankind" Tozer.*

Day 28

Rest in God's Rest

See to it, brothers and sisters, that none of you has a sinful, unbelieving heart that turns away from the living God. But encourage one another daily, as long as it is called "Today," so that none of you may be hardened by sin's deceitfulness. Hebrews 3:12-14

Resting in God's rest is a warning about unbelief. God is who says He is. He will do what He says He will do. And, you are who He says you are.

The writer of Hebrews in Chapter 3 calls us to fix our thoughts on Jesus (v 1). He goes on to warn us about Israel's unbelief and compares our faith to theirs as a caution to fear unbelief and encourage one another to live obediently (v 7-11).

The Israelites were God's chosen people to display His plan for salvation. God promised He would bring them into the land of milk and honey and be with them if they would trust Him and not rebel (Numbers 14:8–9). In Exodus 34:6-7 "The Lord, the Lord, the compassionate and gracious God, slow to anger, abounding in

love and faithfulness, maintaining love to thousands, and forgiving wickedness, rebellion and sin."

Their hearts were always going astray (v 10), and they did not enter His rest (v 11). They didn't believe God to give them a better future. They wanted to go back to Egypt because slavery with good food was preferable to freedom and manna. What did the good news of salvation and future joy profit them? Nothing. They wandered in the wilderness for forty years and were buried there.

Numbers 13 records their unbelief. All they could see were the giants and walled cities. "We seemed like grasshoppers in our own eyes, and we looked the same to them," (v 33). If we rely on ourselves then we are grasshoppers in our own eyes. We are not big enough, strong enough, or clever enough to face the problems and storms of this life. The good news of the gospel is that we don't have to be enough of anything.

We can be like the Israelites thinking back to their days in Egypt. Because they were hungry all they could remember was the food. They failed to recall the time, when the king ordered the midwives to murder all the baby boys. They didn't remember the hours of back breaking work toiling under the hot sun. They didn't remember how the oversees dealt harshly with them. "The Egyptians worked them ruthlessly." (Exodus 1)

Can we be like this? Yes! When we focus our thoughts on solving our problems, we begin to use God for what we can get out of Him. In this world we are going to have troubles. We are going to have diseases, infertility, miscarriages, hurts, and bad habits, etc. We want God to sanctify our wants and just give us our desires. We want solutions more than we want God. Because we are hungry, we want food, and God is giving us Jesus!

After hearing the truth of the gospel, let us not be distracted by our desires, wants, and heartaches. In this life we will face un-fixable situations (John 16:33). My son died. That is permanent. I watched my spiritual mentor die of cancer. That is permanent. A good friend is infertile. That is permanent. We all have faced a giant that made us feel like grasshoppers in our own eyes. God has a long-term strategy to many earthly giants. It's called heaven. My son can't come to me, but I will go to him. As we walk through un-fixable situations our faith changes from fixing our problems to knowing God, and that is what makes heaven all the sweeter.

Rest in God's rest and don't be disqualified by unbelief.

Day 29

Rest in the Compassion of God

*Because of the Lord's great love we are
not consumed, his compassions never fail.
Lamentations 3:22*

In the middle of the messy part of grieving the verse that kept coming to mind is, "Who is this? He commands even the winds and the water, and they obey Him. (Luke 8:25)"

Astonishing! Picture yourself on the boat with the disciples (Luke 8:22-25). The Messiah is asleep. Perhaps at this time the disciples question why Jesus came. Maybe in their panic they fell back on believing He has come to save them from Roman rule and establish His earthly kingdom, and God could conquer the Romans through any one. All they could see were the waves crashing over the sides of the boat. They are drenched both by fear and water.

More than one squall has wreaked havoc in my life that I thought was going to overwhelm me. I wish I could say that my faith was stronger than the disciples. I wish I stood up to the storm and whispered, "God doesn't give the toughest battles to his toughest soldiers. He creates the toughest soldiers through life's hardest battles." I didn't.

I was exactly like the disciples. I prayed and tried to wakeup God as if He were sleeping and took no notice of His little servant.

"Master, Master, we're going to drown!"

Have you been there? Praying and praying and getting no answer. The storm keeps raging. I have. In my weakness, I cried. God didn't make me tough. He showed me His compassion.

In His compassion He whispered, "My grace is sufficient for you, for my power is made perfect in weakness," (2 Corinthians 12:9). I began to understand what Paul was meaning when he wrote, "I delight in weakness, in insults, in hardships, in persecutions, in difficulties. For when I am weak, then I am strong."

I learned that when I want God to set up His Kingdom here and now, fear drenched me because He didn't do what I wanted. His is a Heavenly Kingdom. I enjoy His unfailing compassion because in my weaknesses He has showed me His grace and reminded me that His Kingdom is not of this world.

This world wants tough soldiers, God wants soldiers who depend completely on His compassion. Learning to rest in God's compassion is knowing that by His love we are not consumed. Rest in God's compassion.

Day 30
Rest in the Presence of God

How lovely is your dwelling place, Lord Almighty! My soul yearns, even faints, my heart and my flesh cry out for the living God.
Psalm 84:1-2

Learning to rest in the presence of God is last because I had to learn the lessons of resting in God's plan for redemption first before I came to a place for my heart and flesh to cry out for the living God.

First, we must believe that God demonstrated His love for us though Jesus. Hebrews 11:6, "And without faith it is impossible to please God, because anyone who comes to him must believe that he exists and that he rewards those who earnestly seek him."

Faith is first. Then we must grow in our "knowledge of His will in all wisdom and spiritual understanding so that you may walk worthy of the Lord, fully pleasing to Him (Colossians 1:9)." Then we must rest in repentance and reconciliation. As we know more of who God is we can lay aside our preconceived ideas of God for His Truth.

Today, we hear many people and songs talking about the presence of God. The truth is God is omnipresent. "Nothing in all creation is hidden from God's sight. Everything is uncovered and laid bare before the eyes of him to whom we must give account." (Hebrews 4:13)

In the storm, I released my fantasy of the perfect life. To rest in God's presence, we start with the world as it is. Marriages fail. Babies die. Cancer happens. People lose jobs. People hurt our feelings. Storms come. The storm doesn't define us, and it doesn't change who God is. He doesn't overwhelm us with His presence, so that we involuntarily do the right thing.

The truth is God is always present. We chose whether or not to rest in His presence. Resting takes work. We must know God. In the storm we think that if God rescues us then He's present, and since He hasn't rescued us then He must not be here or care. What our flesh is crying out for is to have a better marriage, have a child, find a miraculous cure for cancer, or get the job back. I admitted to myself and to God that I wanted my child back more than I wanted Him. It was painful. To rest in God's presence, I ask you: Is there something that is keeping you from being satisfied with God alone? Or is it God plus something? If there is a plus, then that is what we truly desire, not God.

We choose. We choose to depend on Him. Hebrews 1:1, "In the past God spoke to our ancestors through the prophets at many times and in many ways, but in these last days he has spoken to us by his Son, whom he appointed heir of all things, and through whom also he made the universe." To rest in God's presence, we must study Jesus and His Scriptures.

Rest in knowing that God is always present. In the storm we can't feel God, but He sees us. He loves us. I leave you with this simple truth that my spiritual mom would always say, "God knows."

Matthea Glass, mother of five, has served alongside her pastor husband, Jon, since 2003. They are currently serving in Birmingham, Alabama. She has a heart for the local church both in the US and globally. Her passion is to see people set free from bondage through her work in Women's Ministry, Celebrate Recovery, and Living Bread Ministries. She blogs at mattheaglass.com.

www.ingramcontent.com/pod-product-compliance
Lightning Source LLC
LaVergne TN
LVHW022325080426
835508LV00013BA/1324